P9-DER-591

D.S.C.

DATE DUE

9.33
88-52

OCT 2 3			
NOV 1 8			
MAR 0 6			
APR 1 4			
MAR 2 1 1994			

984
Bol   Bolivia

Beacon Hill School
Library
Kelso, Washington

Children of the World

Bolívia

For their help in the preparation of *Children of the World: Bolivia,* the editors
gratefully thank Employment and Immigration Canada, Ottawa, Ont.; the US
Immigration and Naturalization Service, Washington, DC; the United States
Department of State, Bureau of Public Affairs, Office of Public Communication,
Washington, DC, for unencumbered use of material in the public domain; and
Ernesto Lopez and Ruth Lopez-Bors, Milwaukee.

Library of Congress Cataloging-in-Publication Data

Ikuhara, Yoshiyuki, 1947-
  Bolivia.

  (Children of the world)
  Bibliography: p.
  Includes index.
  Summary: Presents the life of Porfirio, an Aymara Indian who lives with his family on an
island in Lake Tiricaca, and discusses Bolivia's ethnic groups, religion, government,
education, industry, geography, and history.
  1. Bolivia—Social life and customs—Juvenile literature. 2. Children—Bolivia—Juvenile
literature. [1. Family life—Bolivia. 2. Bolivia—Social life and customs] I. Martin, Michael,
1948-. II. Title. III. Series: Children of the world (Milwaukee, Wis.)
F3310.I39   1989   984   87-42616
ISBN 1-55532-346-4
ISBN 1-55532-321-9 (lib. bdg.)

North American edition first published in 1988 by

Gareth Stevens, Inc.
7317 West Green Tree Road
Milwaukee, Wisconsin 53223, USA

This work was originally published in shortened form consisting of section I only.
Photographs and original text copyright © 1986 by Yoshiyuki Ikuhara.
First and originally published by Kaisei-sha Publishing Co., Ltd., Tokyo.
World English rights arranged with Kaisei-sha Publishing Co., Ltd. through
Japan Foreign-Rights Centre.

Copyright this format © 1988 by Gareth Stevens, Inc.
Additional material and maps copyright © 1988 by Gareth Stevens, Inc.

All rights reserved. No part of this book may be reproduced in any form or by
any means without permission in writing from Gareth Stevens, Inc.

Typeset by Ries Graphics ltd., Milwaukee.
Design: Laurie Bishop.
Map design: Kate Kriege.

1 2 3 4 5 6 7 8 9 93 92 91 90 89 88

Children of the World
Bolivia

Photography by
Yoshiyuki Ikuhara

Edited by
Michael Martin

Beacon Hill School
Library
Kelso, Washington

9.33

Gareth Stevens Publishing
Milwaukee

. . .a note about *Children of the World:*

The children of the world live in fishing towns, Arctic regions, and urban centers, on islands and in mountain valleys, on sheep ranches and fruit farms. This series follows one child in each country through the pattern of his or her life. Candid photographs show the children with their families, at school, at play, and in their communities. The text describes the dreams of the children and, often through their own words, tells how they see themselves and their lives.

Each book also explores events that are unique to the country in which the child lives, including festivals, religious ceremonies, and national holidays. The *Children of the World* series does more than tell about foreign countries. It introduces the children of each country and shows readers what it is like to be a child in that country.

. . .and about *Bolivia:*

Porfirio Esteban is an Aymara Indian who lives with his family on an island in Lake Titicaca, the largest lake in South America. Porfirio and his family live close to the earth, spending much of their time farming and crafting beautiful reed boats. Porfirio's life is much like that of his Indian ancestors in years past — a simple and productive one.

To enhance this book's value in libraries and classrooms, comprehensive reference sections include up-to-date data about Bolivia's geography, demographics, currency, education, culture, industry, and natural resources. *Bolivia* also features a bibliography, research topics, activity projects, and discussions of such subjects as La Paz, the country's history, political system, ethnic and religious composition, and language.

The living conditions and experiences of children in Bolivia vary tremendously according to economic, environmental, and ethnic circumstances. The reference sections help bring to life for young readers the diversity and richness of the culture and heritage of Bolivia. Of particular interest is the sense of time present coexisting in such close proximity to time past — especially as seen in the contrast between life on Porfirio's remote island and the busy pace of a large capital city such as La Paz.

CONTENTS

Porfirio's family and some of their neighbors.

LIVING IN BOLIVIA:
Porfirio, a Boy from the Highlands

Porfirio Esteban is an 11-year-old Aymara Indian boy from Bolivia. He and his family live on Little Suriqui Island in Lake Titicaca, the largest lake in all of South America.

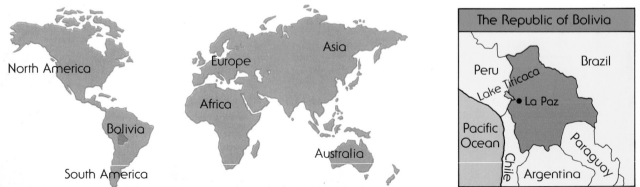

North America

South America

Bolivia

Asia

Europe

Africa

Australia

The Republic of Bolivia

Peru

Lake Titicaca

Brazil

• La Paz

Pacific Ocean

Chile

Paraguay

Argentina

Porfirio lives in an adobe house. Adobes are sun-dried bricks made of mud mixed with straw. He lives there with his parents, Paulino and Maria, his little sister Rosa, his big brother Sergio, and Sergio's wife and baby. Porfirio's father is a master builder of reed boats. Because of his skill, Paulino is famous not only in Bolivia, but all over the world. His picture has even appeared in books.

Porfirio's grandfather and his grandfather's grandfather lived on Little Suriqui Island. In the Aymara language *Suriqui* means "where the birds sleep." Before the Indians came only birds used the island. Today there are about 1,300 people living there. They use boats for fishing and for traveling on the big lake.

One of Porfirio's jobs is to carry water to his house.

Porfirio helps to graze the family's animals.

Sometimes Porfirio gets a ride in the boats his father makes.

The Reed Boats of Lake Titicaca

Lake Titicaca is a very unusual lake. It is more than 12,000 feet (3,800 m) above sea level. That is so high up in the mountains that very few trees can grow there. Since there is so little wood around, the Indians who lived near Lake Titicaca had to find some other material to build boats with.

More than a thousand years ago someone who was very clever discovered a way to make boats out of reeds that grow along the lakeshore. That knowledge was passed down through generations of boat builders until it reached Porfirio's father. Paulino Esteban is one of the very last Aymaras to master the difficult art of building a boat out of reeds.

Today it is much easier to buy wood and bring it over the mountains to Lake Titicaca. Wooden boats are stronger and they last longer, so there will probably not be many more master builders like Porfirio's father.

Paulino shows Porfirio his picture.

A few years ago Paulino helped build a famous boat called the Ra II. A Norwegian explorer believed ancient people could have crossed the ocean using reed boats. In order to prove his theory he asked Porfirio's father and some other Indians to help him build a large boat out of reeds. The boat they made was built so well that it sailed all the way across the Atlantic Ocean.

A model of the boat that crossed the Atlantic.

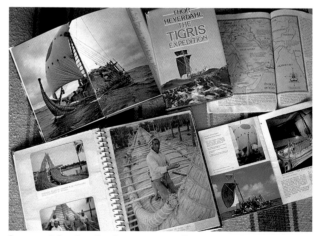
Some of the books that mention Porfirio's father.

Gathering reeds to make a boat.

Building a Balsa de Totora

The whole family helps to gather the reeds that are called "totora." The boats made from these reeds are called "balsa de totora." Every August in Porfirio's village there is a competition to build a reed boat and race it once around Little Suriqui Island. Porfirio is proud because his father won the race last year.

Porfirio's father chooses some of the reeds for the body of the boat. Others he uses to make the rope that will hold the boat together. The rope stretches all the way from the house to the top of a hill. Porfirio gets the important job of rolling up the rope.

It takes about ten days of hard work to make a boat. Water is splashed on the reeds and then they are beaten into shape with a special stone. After that the ropes are pulled tight. It takes great strength and skill. Porfirio helps as much as he can, but he is not strong enough yet for the hardest jobs.

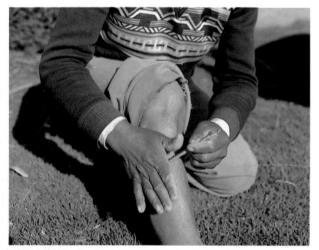
Paulino rolls a reed against his leg to make a rope.

Beginning to roll up the rope.

Working on the boat in the courtyard.

Working on the center of the boat.

Pulling a rope tight.

Shaping the boat.

Sawing wood with Sergio.

Porfirio's brother Sergio makes boats, too. He and some of his friends build boats out of wood because they are stronger than reed boats and can be sold for a higher price. When he grows up Porfirio wants to make both reed boats and wooden boats.

Porfirio's Family at Work

On Little Suriqui Island all the children do their share of the work. Most families are very poor, so people have to work together so that everyone can get enough to eat. Porfirio helps his parents by working around the house and in the fields. Sometimes, when there is lots of work to do, he even gets to skip school.

Little Suriqui Island is so far above sea level that it never gets really hot there. Even on sunny days people usually need extra clothing. At night it often gets very cold. Even while at work, women wear colorful, full skirts one on top of another. On festive occasions they can wear as many as seven skirts. Over their brightly colored blouses, they wear fringed shawls.

Sergio at work.

Indian women work very hard. When she is not making meals, Porfirio's mother works in the corn and potato fields. She also spins yarn and weaves cloth. Sergio's wife, Marta, takes care of her baby, does the wash, and cleans the house. Even Porfirio's little sister Rosa helps by doing housework and taking care of the sheep.

Marta bringing in reeds.

Porfirio's family grows most of the food they eat. Potatoes and corn are their main foods. Though they keep chickens, sheep, and a llama, they rarely eat meat. A big part of their diet comes from the fish they catch in Lake Titicaca.

The whole family eats together twice a day, at sunrise and sunset. After working hard all day, Porfirio can get very hungry. In winter there is less food, so they store and eat dried potatoes called *chuno*.

In the cornfield.

Helping to dig potatoes.

19

Porfirio has to make sure the llama gets enough to eat.

Porfirio's family keeps one llama, eleven sheep, and seven chickens. Every day the sheep have to be taken up in the hills to graze. That job belongs to the women and girls, but Porfirio loves to come along. They usually spend the afternoon up in the mountains with the sheep. At noon they may eat something simple, like a potato. If they are thirsty, all they have to do is scoop up spring water with their hats.

Taking the sheep to pasture. ▶

Meals at Porfirio's House

Porfirio eats lots of potatoes. Sometimes he has potatoes for breakfast, lunch, and supper. Often his mother boils the potatoes with a fish called *carachi* to make a kind of soup. Corn and beans can also be added to the soup. Since the Aymaras do not eat meat very often, the little fish make a tasty addition to their diet.

Porfirio eating breakfast.

Another meal of potatoes.

Porfirio's married older sister lives next door.

Most of the family eats sitting on the floor. Each person has a plate of soup. They all help themselves to the fish and potatoes. Today there is plenty, but this is not always the case. Many people in Bolivia go to bed hungry.

Cornmeal is used to make the base for a thick and nutritious soup. Meat — sheep and llama — is preserved by sun-drying it with salt in thin slices. It is too expensive to eat often.

Eating supper together.

Porfirio's School

There is only one elementary school on Little Suriqui Island. It takes Porfirio about five minutes to walk there from his house. If he has work to do in the morning he will not go to school until the afternoon.

The school is right beside the lake.

Porfirio's school is the white building on the left.

Porfirio's 5th grade class.

Porfirio's teacher is Mr. Gerbesio. The children do not have any books. Books are supposed to be provided free of charge, but the Bolivian government cannot afford schoolbooks for the country's children. Since the children have no notebooks or pencils, they never have anything to carry to school. Also, many students are absent each day because their parents need them to work in the fields.

Mr. Gerbesio draws a problem on a student's desk.

Spanish is the official language of Bolivia, but sometimes Mr. Gerbesio speaks Aymara to the children because he knows they do not understand Spanish well. Porfirio has to listen carefully since he cannot write anything down. School lasts from nine in the morning until four in the afternoon, and there is a 2½ hour break for lunch.

Two children sit at each desk.

Talking about plants in science class.

Children working with clay.

Porfirio's class with the figures they made out of clay.

In the afternoon the children have a crafts class. Sometimes they make things with clay. The girls make dolls or stoves while the boys make animals or boats. Porfirio decides to make a boat like the ones his father builds.

The children always have lots of fun making things in crafts class. That makes Mr. Gerbesio a little sad. He wishes the school could afford to buy more clay so Porfirio and his classmates could practice more often.

The boys make boats or animals.

The boys playing soccer.

Recess.

The first game of tug-of-war ends suddenly!

In his physical education class Porfirio gets to play soccer. The school only has one soccer ball, so the different grades take turns using it. Sometimes the ball goes into the lake. Then one of the boys has to climb into a boat and go get it.

After soccer the boys play a tug-of-war game. They draw a line between the two teams. Whichever team pulls the other over the line wins. It is hard to win because their hands often slip apart, but everyone has a good time anyway.

The boys try again. Hanging on is tough.

Life on Suriqui Island

There are no doctors where Porfirio lives. Many of the Aymara still use herbs and magic charms against diseases. The nearest large town is six hours away by boat. Little Suriqui has no electricity and no cars, either. After the sun goes down it becomes very quiet and dark there.

Luisa, the town nurse.

The open air market. Electric wires still hang overhead, though the island's generator no longer works.

Tuesday is the most exciting day of the week for Porfirio. That is when the open-air market called the Feria is held. Merchants come by boat from other islands and from Peru to the plaza in front of the church. There they sell vegetables, fruits, pottery, candles, and all kinds of things that the people of Suriqui cannot normally buy. Porfirio visits the plaza before school starts and again during his 2½ hour lunch break.

The Feria is the most important social event of the week for the people of Suriqui. It gives them a chance to meet old friends and make new ones, many of them Peruvians. Most of the merchants sleep overnight in their boats before moving on to another island the next morning.

Meeting friends from Peru.

Dancing the *chotas*.

Porfirio's homemade bow-and-arrow.

Eating *tuna*, a fruit from a cactus.

Chickens are hard to catch.

Some of the merchants at the Feria sell candy. Porfirio loves chocolate, but his parents can only buy it for him two or three times a year. Sometimes his big brother Sergio will buy him chocolate. When Porfirio and his friends are happy they do a dance called the *chotas*. The Aymaras use the *chotas* to ask God for a good harvest.

Besides Little Suriqui Island there are about 40 other islands in Lake Titicaca. The lake is a sacred place to the Indians of Bolivia. According to their legends, it was there that the great god Viracocha rose and spread knowledge to the peoples who lived in the Andes Mountains.

Along the shores of the lake and on some of the islands are the ruins of stone temples and buildings. They are some of the oldest ruins in all of the Americas. They were probably made by Porfirio's ancestors, but they were built so long ago that no one knows for sure.

Island women doing their washing in the lake.

Indian women with *ahuayos* on their backs.

The Indians of Bolivia dress very colorfully. The women wear bright colored clothes and bowler hats. They use a single piece of cloth called an *ahuayo* (also spelled *aguayo*) to carry heavy loads on their backs. When they carry babies in their *ahuayos* they tie the cloth very tight to keep the baby's soul from escaping.

Beacon Hill School
Library
Kelso, Washington

Nights get very cold.

Looking at Sergio's book.

Practicing writing.

Porfirio's Day

Porfirio goes to bed when it gets dark and gets up at sunrise. After he gets up he usually goes out to work in the fields or to fish in the lake. When his chores are done Porfirio eats breakfast and goes to school.

When there is lots of work to do Porfirio has to stay home and help out. His father believes education is important, so he only has Porfirio stay home to work when he can't get along without him.

Today is a day of great luxury for Porfirio. He has a banana! Bananas are grown far off in the valley or *yungas*. Transporting them between the *yungas* and Lake Titicaca makes them very rare and expensive.

Eating a precious banana.

When Porfirio gets home from school he usually has more work to do. One of his jobs is to carry water to the house. Spring water is brought down the mountainside to five locations in the village. Then children with buckets fetch the water from community faucets.

Sometimes, when he has nothing to do, Porfirio sneaks into Sergio's room to look at his books. When Porfirio plays with his friends they make bows and slingshots. He especially likes playing war with slingshots. They shoot little nuts at each other. It hurts when you get hit, but it is still fun.

Fetching water.

Sergio plays the accordion.

Today Sergio has just sold the boat he and his friends built. He decides to celebrate. That night the neighbors gather for a party. Sergio plays the accordion while Porfirio and Rosa dance. The party lasts until late at night, and everyone has a good time.

This accordion was a gift to Porfirio's father from some foreigners he worked with on the Ra expedition. The people of Suriqui are otherwise very unlikely to have an instrument like this or anything else that must be imported because of the great cost.

Singing with a friend.

Dancing with Rosa.

The village where Porfirio lives.

La Paz

Bolivia has two capitals. The city of Sucre was declared the capital when the republic was founded. However, the seat of government is in La Paz, and most people consider it to be the capital of the country.

Although La Paz is only about 50 miles (80 km) east of Lake Titicaca, Porfirio has never been there. La Paz has a population of about 800,000 and is the highest capital city in the world. There are many modern buildings standing near other buildings that are hundreds of years old. The churches, especially, are quite old.

The city is a mixture of old and modern buildings.

Even though La Paz is built at the bottom of a valley, the downtown area is still 12,000 feet (3,700 m) above sea level. Because it is so far up in the mountains, people who are not used to living there often have trouble breathing the thin air. The airport and the hotels keep oxygen tanks nearby to help visitors who get sick. Usually it takes about three days for people to get used to the altitude.

Downtown La Paz.

On Sagarnaga Street in La Paz is a famous market run by local merchants. These small stores cater to tourists by selling typical Bolivian handicrafts — knitted and woven clothes and blankets, leather, pewter, and copper goods, and much more. Most of the merchants are *mestizo*, a mixture of Spanish and Indian blood. Sometimes Indian vendors come to sell their silver artifacts. They sit on the ground and spread their wares out in front of them. If you listen closely you can hear words in Aymara, Quechua, and other Indian languages flying back and forth, but the main language of the market is Spanish.

Old houses and narrow streets.

An Indian woman with her ahuayo.

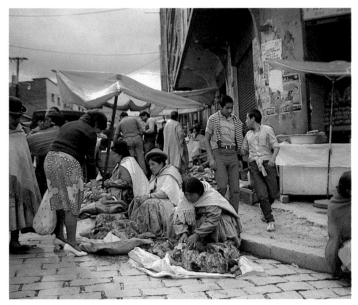

The Indian market.

A view of the city from a mountaintop.

La Paz has grown up the mountainside in the shape of a bowl. Most of the streets and paths between buildings are very steep. Children run up and down the hills or sell gum and chocolate in tiny shops. Indians come and go in the traditional clothing of their tribes. The buses carrying them are almost always full.

Porfirio would like to visit La Paz someday, but he wants to live on Little Suriqui Island. If all goes as he plans, he will grow up there and build boats like his brother and his father before him.

FOR YOUR INFORMATION: Bolivia

Official Name: Republic of Bolivia
República de Bolivia
[Ray-POO-blee-kah deh Bo-LEE-vee-ah]

Capital: La Paz

History

The Aymara and the Incas

The original inhabitants of Bolivia were Indians. Between 100 BC and AD 600 it is believed that Aymara Indians living near the southern end of Lake Titicaca produced a highly advanced culture. The remains of that culture can still be seen today around the shores of the lake. At Tiahuanacuo lie the ruins of mighty stone temples and buildings. People come from all over the world to visit them. However, very little is known of the mysterious people who built Tiahuanacuo.

About the middle of the 15th century Inca armies from what is now Peru moved into the Bolivian highlands. The Incas built hundreds of miles of roads through the Andes, and their armies were highly skilled. They defeated the Aymara and other local tribes in fierce fighting. Even after their defeat, the Aymara stubbornly fought to

A relic of Tiahuanacuo.

preserve their own culture. That is why they still speak their own language today while most of Bolivia's other Indians now speak Quechua.

The Colonial Period

When the Spanish began their conquest of Peru and Bolivia in 1532, the Incas were weakened by a civil war. That made it possible for a relatively small number of Spanish soldiers to triumph. The Indians fought bravely, but they were no match for the armor, steel, and horses of the Spanish.

Spain ruled Bolivia for nearly 300 years. During that time the country was called Upper Peru. The colony soon became very important because of the rich deposits of silver discovered there. The richest of them all was the "mountain of silver" around which the city of Potosi sprang up. Silver was discovered there in 1545. Within a few years 100,000 people were gathered around the mines. The deposits were so large that the Spanish government had minting equipment shipped to Potosi from Spain. As soon as the silver came out of the ground it was made into bars and coins.

For more than a century Potosi was the richest and largest city in all of the Americas. By 1650 the population was more than 150,000. Hundreds of millions of dollars worth of silver were sent back to Spain. The mine owners became fabulously wealthy while the Indians living in the mountains around Potosi were forced to work in the mines as slaves. The Spanish set up a hated labor system called the *mita*. It required male Indians from each village to work in the mines for a set period of time, usually a year. Thousands of Indians died from the cruel conditions in the mines and from diseases caught from the Europeans.

Indian uprisings were common in Bolivia during the period of Spanish rule, but none were successful. The last major uprising occurred around La Paz in 1780. It was led by an Indian who claimed to be a descendant of the Incas. After a series of bloody battles the Indians were completely crushed in 1783.

Independence

In 1809 Pedro Domingo Murillo led a revolt against the Spanish. He was successful in gaining control of La Paz, but he was captured during a counterattack by government troops. In 1810 Murillo was hanged in the central plaza of La Paz. His followers continued to fight on until their country was freed in 1825. Bolivians consider Murillo to be the father of their country's independence.

Simón Bolívar, the man for whom Bolivia is named, was responsible for finally driving the Spanish out of South America. Two of his generals, Antonio José de Sucre and Andrés de Santa Cruz, played major roles in winning Bolivia's independence. Santa Cruz and his soldiers attacked La Paz in 1823 and did much damage to the Spanish troops there. A year later Bolívar defeated the Spanish in a decisive battle in Peru. Afterwards he sent General Sucre to Bolivia to drive the Spanish from that area. Sucre was successful, and independence was officially proclaimed on August 6, 1825. On that day Upper Peru became Bolivia.

Growth of the new country was very slow because Bolivia's leaders were so busy fighting for power among themselves. They had little time or energy left for governing wisely. In 1879 Bolivia and Chile went to war over who should control the seacoast west of Bolivia. The war was a disaster because Bolivia lost its seaport on the Pacific Ocean. One reason that Bolivia's development has been so slow is that there is no cheap way to ship goods into or out of the country.

The Chaco War

Although Bolivia had lost its seacoast, the 50 years following the Pacific War were relatively good times for the country. World prices for metals mined in Bolivia remained high. Things began to change for the worse in the 1930s. To the south of Bolivia is a dry, desertlike region called the Gran Chaco. From 1932 until 1935 Bolivia and Paraguay fought a war over who would control this region. It is thought that wealthy Bolivians began the war in order to capture ports on the Paraguay River. That river eventually empties into the Atlantic Ocean.

The Chaco War is considered one of the turning points in Bolivian history. Indians were forced to do most of the fighting, and thousands died. The Bolivian army was unprepared to deal with the heat, insects, and tropical diseases of the lowlands. Civilian and military leaders performed very badly during the war, and as many as 100,000 Bolivians may have died. Bolivia was a much larger country, yet when the war was over it had lost much territory to the Paraguayans. The experience created a desire among Indians and other powerless people to change the way their country was run. That goal was finally achieved in 1952.

The Revolution of 1952

The Bolivian revolution of 1952 is considered one of the most important Latin American revolutions of this century. It was responsible for many positive changes in the country. The size of the army was reduced, everyone was given the right to vote, and the Indians were given land and political power. Projects were begun to provide poor people living in the countryside with education and medical care.

Unfortunately, the army was allowed to regain its former size and, in 1964, it again overthrew the elected government. Since then there have been more than a dozen presidents, most of them military men who seized power by force.

The People — Population and Ethnic Groups

Bolivia is the least heavily populated country in South America. According to the latest estimates, between six and seven million people live there. And of all the

South American countries, Bolivia has the highest percentage of Indians. They make up 55% of the population, while people of Spanish or other European descent account for only 15% of the total. The remaining 30% of the people are of mixed Spanish and Indian blood. Although 85% of its people are either Indian or part Indian, Bolivia has traditionally been a country where power and wealth have been concentrated in the hands of people of Spanish descent.

The Aymara

The shores of Lake Titicaca and the plains that surround them are the natural homeland of the Aymara Indians. There are about 1½ million Aymara living in Bolivia. In recent years the Aymara have been moving to the cities, especially to La Paz. Still, those Aymara who remain in the countryside continue to speak their own language and live much the same way their ancestors did hundreds of years ago.

Much of the land the Aymara live on is very poor. It takes a lot of work to grow enough food to survive in that harsh environment. The main crops are barley, potatoes, beans, and onions. Where grass grows, llamas, sheep, and alpacas are grazed. The Aymara make their own clothes from the wool they collect from their animals. They rarely eat meat because they cannot afford to kill their animals. Fish they catch in Lake Titicaca are an important addition to their diet.

Aymara children are expected to be quiet, hard-working, and polite. Their parents are usually loving and protective in return. Although the children go to government schools, they are also expected to help their parents whenever there is much work to be done. In a way, the Aymara are people without a past. Where they came from and how they arrived in the Lake Titicaca region is a mystery. It is thought that the Aymara were responsible for the advanced civilization which built cities like Tiahuanacuo. Though they have little memory of the past, the Aymara are certain to play a role in Bolivia's future.

The Quechuas

Just under two million Quechuas live in Bolivia. Like the Aymara, the Quechua have their own language. The Quechua, however, have a greater sense of their past. Quechua was the language spoken by the Incas, the people who invaded Bolivia before the arrival of the Spanish.

The Quechua live and eat in much the same manner as other Bolivian Indians, but their villages are organized very differently. In that organization one can see the influence of the Incas. For example, the Incas used a labor system called the *ayni*. Instead of each family working alone in its own fields, the whole village worked on each of its member's fields in turn. The Quechua still practice that system today. Life is hard for the Quechua, but because everyone experiences the good times and the hard times together, it does not seem so bad. Quechuas who move away to the cities usually remain poor, and they often lose that feeling of working and suffering together. Some of them become depressed and disappointed and turn to drinking. One of the problems Bolivia faces is finding a way to improve the living conditions of its Indians without destroying the positive things about their cultures.

The Chipayas and the Kallawayas

The Chipaya are an ancient people whose unusual way of life may provide clues to understanding the mysterious ruins left by earlier civilizations in the Andes. They have broader faces and darker skins than the Aymara, and they speak a very old language called Uru-Chipaya.

The Chipaya live on the desertlike salt flats which lie to the south of Lake Titicaca. Their houses are completely round and have no windows. The small doorways always face away from the prevailing wind. The ancient peoples of Bolivia buried their dead in towers that look very much like the round houses of the Chipaya. Their land cannot grow many crops so, unlike other highland Indians, the Chipaya get much of their food by hunting. They use the *bolas,* a Y-shaped cord with lead weights on two ends and a light stone on the other. There are salt lakes near where the Chipaya live, and they go there to hunt birds like the flamingo. After stalking a group of flamingoes, a Chipaya hunter will twirl the bolas above his head and then throw it. If he is lucky the whirling cords will tangle in the bird's legs and it will fall to the ground where it can easily be killed. There are fewer than a thousand Chipaya left in Bolivia, and their unique culture is in danger of disappearing.

The Kallawaya live in an isolated area in the mountains to the east of Lake Titicaca. They are close neighbors with the Aymara and are famous throughout the Andes for their healing and curing powers. In the Aymara language Kallawaya means to "carry medicine on the shoulder." The Kallawaya know much about the plants that grow in Bolivia, and they use that knowledge to help other Indians. Kallawaya doctors travel to mountain villages carrying dried herbs in cloth bags.

Besides speaking Spanish, Quechua, and Aymara, the Kallawaya have their own secret language which they use when they are practicing their medicine. Few outsiders have been allowed to visit Kallawaya villages, and little is known of their culture. It is possible they have knowledge of plants unknown to modern science, plants which could prove useful in fighting diseases. That has happened before. When the Spanish arrived in South America, they found the Indians using the bark of a tree as medicine to cure malaria. Today that tree is recognized as the source of the valuable drug quinine.

The Cholos

In Bolivia, people of mixed blood are called *mestizo.* Some belong to the social class called *Cholo.* Because they are neither pure Spanish nor pure Indian, Cholos have been looked down upon by both groups. People used to say that Cholos had lost the qualities of the Indian and gained nothing from the Spanish.

52

The outlook for Cholo children used to be a life of hardship and discrimination. Today the future looks much brighter. Because of their unique position in Bolivian society many Cholos speak both Spanish and Indian languages. Their ability to communicate with both groups has increased their importance.

Their talents will probably be needed more as the Indians play a greater role in the social life of their country. Many Cholos have found work in the government while others run small shops or businesses. In La Paz the street markets are run by Cholo women called *Cholas*. They dress and look just like ordinary Indian women, but some of them have become quite wealthy. Today, Cholo children have a better chance of growing up and living successful lives.

Language

Spanish has long been the official language of Bolivia, but in reality there are three major languages. The other two are Aymara and Quechua. People like the Cholos who can speak more than one language have an advantage in Bolivian society.

Education

Bolivia's wealthy landowners used to be responsible for educating the people living on their lands. Most of them had little interest in seeing the Indians learn Spanish, so most Indian children grew up illiterate. The revolution of 1952 greatly changed the way Bolivian children were educated. Before that time only 15% of the children who lived in the countryside went to school. Since 1952 the percentage has risen to about 80%. Even so, Bolivia maintains two separate school systems, one for the people living out in the country and one for everyone else. The law says that children must go to school between the ages of 7 and 14. That law is not very strictly enforced, especially in rural areas where Indian children often drop out of school to help their parents. Of the children who complete grade school, only one out of three goes to high school.

After 1952 the government promised to provide a teacher and learning materials for any school built by the Indians. That promise led to an increase in the number of schools in small towns and remote areas. Many rural Indians saw education as a way out of their poverty but there are still many problems. One is a shortage of good teachers who are willing to work and live away from the big cities. And classes are usually taught in Spanish, a language Indian children do not always understand. Recently some classes have been taught using Indian languages.

There are eight public universities in Bolivia. The largest is the University of San Andrés in La Paz with 17,000 students. The university in Sucre is one of the oldest in the Americas, founded in 1624. College graduates from all levels of society are increasing, but many more will be needed if Bolivia is to have a brighter future.

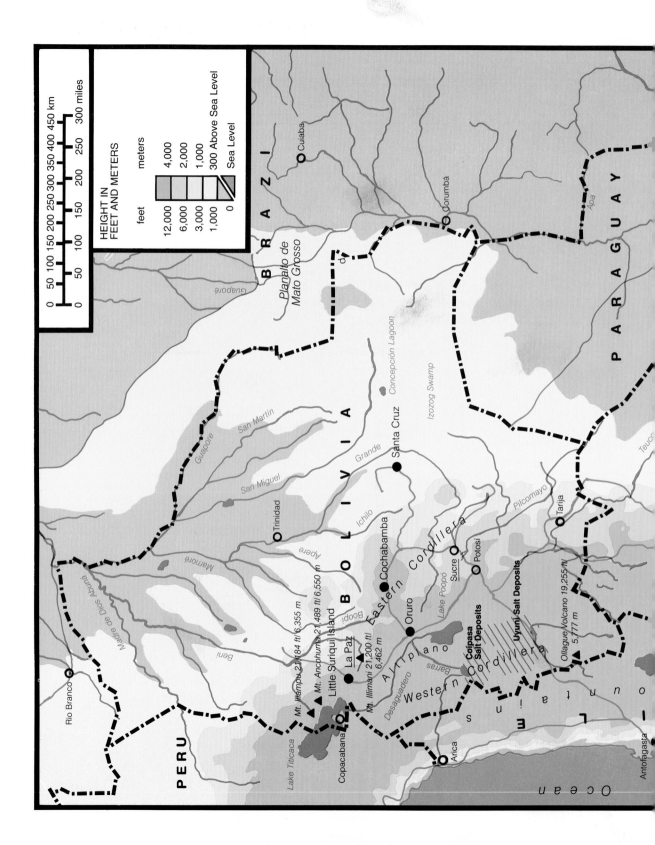

HEIGHT IN FEET AND METERS

feet	meters
12,000	4,000
6,000	2,000
3,000	1,000
1,000	300 Above Sea Level
0	Sea Level

0 50 100 150 200 250 300 350 400 450 km

0 50 100 150 200 250 300 miles

BRAZIL

PERU

PARAGUAY

BOLIVIA

Cuiaba

Corumbá

Apa

Guaporé

Planalto de Mato Grosso

Concepción Lagoon

Izozog Swamp

San Martín

Santa Cruz

Grande

Teuco

Ichilo

Pilcomayo

Tarija

Cochabamba

San Miguel

Trinidad

Apere

Mamoré

Guaporé

Eastern Cordillera

Cordillera

Oruro

Sucre

Potosí

Lake Poopó

Uyuni Salt Deposits

Coipasa Salt Deposits

Ollague Volcano 19,255 ft/ 5,777 m

Madre de Dios Abuná

Rio Branco

Beni

Beni

Boopi

La Paz

Mt. Illampu 21,484 ft/ 6,355 m

Mt. Ancohuma 21,489 ft/ 6,550 m

Little Suriqui Island

Mt. Illimani 21,200 ft/ 6,462 m

Altiplano

Desaguadero

Barras

Western Cordillera

Mountains

Lake Titicaca

Copacabana

Arica

Antofagasta

Ocean

BOLIVIA — Political and Physical

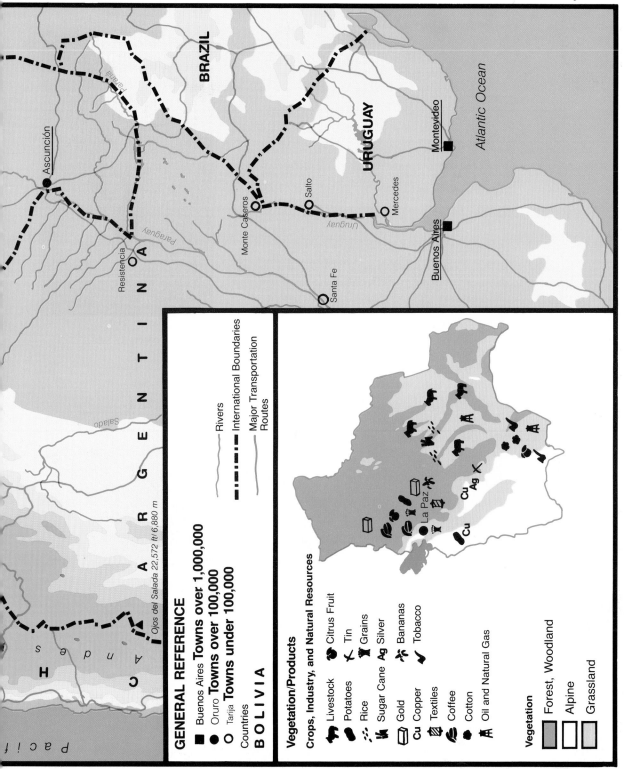

BRAZIL

URUGUAY

Atlantic Ocean

Montevideo

Ascunción

Salto

Monte Caseros

Mercedes

Buenos Aires

Resistencia

Santa Fe

Paraguay

Uruguay

Paraná

A R G E N T I N A

Salado

Andes

Ojos del Salada 22,572 ft/6,880 m

Pacif

La Paz

BOLIVIA

Cu

Cu

Ag

GENERAL REFERENCE

Buenos Aires **Towns over 1,000,000**
Oruro **Towns over 100,000**
Tarija **Towns under 100,000**
Countries

Rivers
International Boundaries
Major Transportation Routes

Vegetation/Products

Crops, Industry, and Natural Resources

Livestock
Potatoes
Rice
Sugar Cane
Gold
Cu Copper
Textiles
Coffee
Cotton

Citrus Fruit
Tin
Grains
Ag Silver
Bananas
Tobacco
Oil and Natural Gas

Vegetation

Forest, Woodland
Alpine
Grassland

The Land

Bolivia is the fifth largest country in South America with an area of 424,165 square miles (1,098,581 sq km), about the size of Texas and California combined. It is a landlocked country, bordered on the north and east by Brazil, on the south by Paraguay and Argentina, and on the west by Chile and Peru. Bolivia has been nicknamed the "rooftop of the world," but it is more than a country of majestic, snowcapped mountains. There are also deserts, forests, prairies, and dense tropical jungles. They occur in three distinct regions.

A cantuta, the Bolivian national flower.

The Western Highlands

The Andes are the longest mountain range in the world, and they contain some of the highest peaks and most magnificent scenery anywhere. In Bolivia they run from north to south in two parallel ranges. The Western Cordillera, also known as the Cordillera Occidental, forms the country's border with Chile. The Eastern Cordillera, or Cordillera Real, marks the eastern boundary of the highlands. Both mountain ranges are extremely high with many peaks over 16,000 feet (4,800 m) and a few over 20,000 feet (6,000 m). Many of the peaks are snowcapped year round, and a number of them are active volcanoes. Between the two mountain ranges at a height of about 12,000 feet (3,650 m) lies a cold, dry plateau called the Altiplano (high plain). The Altiplano has an average width of about 80 miles (130 km). Though the climate is harsh, most of Bolivia's people live there.

The Eastern Foothills

The eastern slopes of the Cordillera Real drop sharply toward Bolivia's lowland plains. In this area are steep-sided valleys and rolling hills. The warm, fertile valleys at lower altitudes are called *yungas*. The important cities of Sucre, Cochabamba, and Tarija are all located in yungas. There are heavy forests and few roads in much of this region. Travel between valleys is often difficult.

The Oriente

The warm, flat lands of the Oriente, or Eastern Lowlands, make up nearly two-thirds of Bolivia's area. Yet, until recently, almost no one lived there. The discovery of oil and natural gas and the construction of new roads are beginning to change that situation. The government has been trying to encourage Bolivians from the crowded highlands to move to the prairies and plains of the Oriente.

Climate

As might be expected, Bolivia has quite a variety of climates. The Altiplano is cool, dry, and windy all year long with little difference between the seasons. Temperatures often reach into the 60s F (15-18°C) during the day while, at night, they frequently drop below freezing. Lake Titicaca is such a large lake that is has an effect on the climate of the highlands. The areas near the lake receive up to five times as much rainfall as the southern Altiplano.

Because of their lesser altitude, the foothills on the eastern slopes of the Cordillera Real are considerably warmer than the highlands. The northern foothills are humid and wet, while those further south are cooler and more pleasant. Some say they have the most pleasant climate in Bolivia. During the winter months of June, July, and August, people from the highlands sometimes visit the southern *yungas*, or valleys, to escape the cold winds of the Altiplano.

In general, the lowlands have a tropical climate. Heavy rains and warm temperatures in the north help support the thick jungles which form part of the Amazon River basin. Rainfall gradually decreases toward the southern end of the Oriente. In the Chaco region of the extreme south, rivers flow strongly only during the rainy season. There may be no rain at all during the rest of the year.

Industry

Bolivia is the world's second largest exporter of tin. Even though only 3% of the population is involved in mining, it is the country's only large industry.

Unfortunately, the health of the economy depends on things that happen outside Bolivia. When the world prices for tin fall, as they did in the early 1980s, the whole country suffers. The government hopes that the development of oil and natural gas reserves will make the Bolivian economy more stable in the future. It is also encouraging farming in the relatively unpopulated lowlands.

Another big problem for industry is the lack of coal and hydroelectric power. Manufacturing plants need cheap sources of energy. They also need people who can afford to buy their goods. In the past Bolivia's Indians made all their own clothes and furniture. That is slowly changing, but most Indians will need to improve their positions in society before they can buy more goods.

Natural Resources

Bolivia has the potential to be a very wealthy country. Its resources include tin, silver, and many other metals in the mountains; oil and natural gas in the lowlands; and great forests in the lower valleys. Because of its geography, Bolivia cannot take full advantage of its resources. It is blocked by the Cordillera Occidental to the west and by long stretches of uninhabited land to the north and east.

Agriculture

More than half of all Bolivians farm the land. Raising enough food to eat is a difficult task in much of Bolivia, especially in the highlands, or Altiplano. The most important farming area in the Altiplano is along the shores of Lake Titicaca. Major crops grown there are potatoes, and quinoa and barley, both grains. These are among the few plants that will grow at such a high altitude.

The most fertile areas in Bolivia are the valleys and foothills on the eastern slopes of the Cordillera Real. Crops include citrus fruits, coffee, bananas, corn, wheat, and tobacco. Coffee is grown in enough quantity to be shipped to other countries. Major lowland crops include rice, cotton, and sugar cane.

A plant with shiny green leaves grows wild in many parts of Bolivia. The plant is called *coca*, and for thousands of years the Indians have chewed its leaves. Their lives are hard and they often have to work when they are cold and hungry. Coca helps them do their work by numbing their senses to the cold and deadening their appetites. But when treated with the right kinds of chemicals, coca can be turned into the illegal drug cocaine. In fact, much of the cocaine that makes its way to North America and Europe comes from illegal laboratories in Bolivia.

It is a problem that the governments of Bolivia and the United States have been working together to solve. In 1986, United States military forces went to Bolivia to help the government find and destroy the places where cocaine was being made. They were successful in destroying large amounts of cocaine and many of the laboratories where it was made. Recently the US government has cut economic assistance to Bolivia because it does not feel the Bolivian government is doing enough to stop the growth and export of cocaine.

Government

The city of Sucre, named after General Sucre, was designated Bolivia's capital in 1825. Today the major government offices are located in La Paz, and it is considered Bolivia's real capital.

Bolivia has been one of the most unstable countries in the world. Since its independence in 1825 there have been more than 190 changes of government. Usually these changes occurred because wealthy landowners and military men were fighting for power among themselves. Rarely have Bolivians had leaders who were interested in making their country a better place for everyone. Indians were never even allowed to vote until after the revolution in 1952. Today they are slowly learning how to gain and use political power.

The latest constitution was written in 1967 and, like the United States constitution and the original Bolivian constitution, it provides for three branches of government: the executive, legislative, and judicial. The executive branch under the direction of the president is by far the strongest branch of government.

Bolivia is divided into nine departments. These are the equivalent of states in the United States or provinces in Canada. The heads of each department are appointed by the central government. As a result of the 1985 elections Bolivian citizens can elect their own mayors and city councils.

Currency

Since 1987, the *Boliviano* has replaced the *peso* as the standard unit of currency.

Religion

Almost 95% of Bolivians are Roman Catholics, the religion brought to South America by the Spanish. However, religion as practiced in many parts of the country is a mixture of Christian and native Indian beliefs. God is often associated with the sun, the Virgin Mary with Pachamamma, Mother Earth, and the saints with the spirits who live in the mountains. Before drinking, many Indians will pour a few drops on the ground and ask Pachamamma to drink with them.

Every Indian village has its own patron saint whose fiesta is celebrated annually. Every year a different person is chosen to pay for the fiesta. It's an expensive duty, but one people proudly accept. The ceremonies are mostly Catholic with much feasting, drinking, and dancing.

Art and Culture

In the culture of modern Bolivia one can see a combination of Spanish and Indian influences. For example, the Indians of the Andes were mining and working gold and silver long before the arrival of the Spanish. After the Spanish came, those skills were used to produce religious art. The Indians have always made most of their own clothing. The weaving done by Bolivian women is some of the finest in the world. Beautifully designed and colored hats, blankets, and robes are made everywhere in the highlands. Most Indians outside the cities, especially women, can be identified by the type of clothing they wear. Each region uses its own particular colors and designs.

The alpaca is a camel-like animal that looks like a sheep with a long neck. Alpaca wool is of a very high quality, finer than a sheep's. When spun and woven, it is warm and soft. Baby alpaca wool is even softer, and very expensive. The Indians have been making clothing from Alpaca wool for centuries. In La Paz several small factories have been set up to produce and export fine alpaca sweaters, shawls, and skirts to other countries. Some of the designs on these clothes are more than a thousand years old. These designs appear on the ruins at Tiahuanacuo.

Bolivian popular music varies from region to region. Spanish influence in music is strongest in the lowlands. There, dances like the tango, the bolero, and the *bailecito* are popular. In the highlands the Indians dance to music played on instruments they make themselves. Two of the native instruments used are the flute, or *queno*, and the *charango*, a guitar made out of an armadillo shell. In general, the music of the lowlands is fast and lively, while the music of the highlands is sad and lonely sounding. Some have said that highland Indian music sounds like the cold winds that blow across the Altiplano during the winter.

Sports and Recreation

Bolivians love soccer, which they call football. Even the poorest children play soccer in the streets with ragballs, balls made from old cloth. Basketball and volleyball are also popular in the schools. Sports in Bolivia are more for recreation than competition. There are some professional teams, but players usually hold other jobs.

For the wealthy, the world's highest golf course is at Malasilla. A golf ball soars much farther here at 11,000 feet (3,330 m) above sea level than it would at lower altitudes. Mt. Chacaltaya, at 15,224 feet (4,567 m) above sea level, is the world's highest ski slope. Some skiers, mostly tourists, carry oxygen tanks on their backs because the air is so thin they could tire easily or become ill. This altitude sickness is called *soroche*. Often it affects people by making them very tired and causing terrible headaches. After about three days the symptoms go away, but it can take about six months for a person to become physically attuned to the high altitude.

Strictly for natives or those completely adjusted to the altitude is a winter event at Lake Titicaca. At the narrowest point of the lake, swimmers coat themselves with grease and race across the strait. With the water at 51°F (10°C), it is a race for the strong and quick.

La Paz

Most of La Paz lies between 11,000 and 12,000 feet (3,350-3,655 m) above sea level. With a population of about a million, it is usually considered the world's highest big city. It is certainly a city with spectacular natural beauty. The sky is usually a deep shade of blue and just to the north and east the snow-covered peaks of the Cordillera Real rise to well over 20,000 feet (6,000 m). The two tallest peaks that can be seen from La Paz are called Illampu and Illimani.

The city was founded in 1548 by the Spanish. Its name means "peace" in Spanish, but La Paz has not had a peaceful history. La Paz grew because it is at the center of Bolivia's transportation routes. It is a major stop on the famous Pan American highway which links Lima, Peru, and Buenos Aires, Argentina. Railroads run to other parts of Bolivia and to ports in Chile and Argentina. High on a plateau above the city is the suburb of El Alto. The airport there connects La Paz with other important South American cities.

The center of the city is the central square called the Plaza Murillo. Around it are important buildings like the presidential palace, the congressional palace, and the Roman Catholic cathedral. Besides being the commercial center of Bolivia, La Paz is also the cultural center. The city has many libraries and museums of art, archaeology, and folk art.

Bolivians in North America

Each year, about 1,000 people leave Bolivia to live in the United States. Between 40 and 50 go to Canada. Over half of these immigrants are younger than 30. Most Bolivians maintain strong ties to their homeland. Though its climate is harsh and many have left to escape poverty, the country holds fast to the hearts of its people. Those who can return often to visit family left behind.

More Books About Bolivia

Here are some books about Bolivia. If you are interested in them, check your library. Some may help you do research for the projects that follow.

How the Birds Changed their Feathers: A South American Folk Tale. Troughton
   (Bedrick Books)
Incas. Beck (Franklin Watts)
South America. Carter (Franklin Watts)
South America. Sabin (Troll)

Glossary of Useful Bolivian (Spanish) Terms

adobe (ah-DOH-be) . . . . bricks made out of sun-dried mud
aguayo or ahuayo (ah-GWAH-yo). . . . . a square of brightly colored material
                                            twisted into a carrying pouch
Altiplano (ahl-tee-PLAH-no) . . . . the high, arid plains in western Bolivia
                                            which lie between the Cordillera Real and
                                            the Cordillera Occidental
bolas (BOH-lahss) . . . . a Y-shaped cord with weights tied on the
                                            ends, used for hunting
charango (chah-RANG-go) . . . . a guitar made out of armadillo shells
chicha (CHEE-chah) . . . . alcoholic drink made from Indian corn
pollera (po-LAIR-ah) . . . . a colorful skirt worn by Indian women
sierra (see-AIR-ah) . . . . a range of mountains or hills with jagged or
                                            sawlike ridges
yungas (YOONG-gass) . . . . narrow, steep-sided valleys on the eastern
                                            slopes of the Cordillera Real

Things to Do — Research Projects

Governments can change leadership suddenly in Bolivia. It has had more than a dozen presidents since 1964. As you read about Bolivia, keep in mind the importance of current facts. Some of the research projects that follow need accurate, up-to-date information from current sources. Two publications in your library will tell you about recent newspaper and magazine articles on many topics.

The Reader's Guide to Periodical Literature
Children's Magazine Guide

For answers to questions about such topics of current interest as Bolivia's cocaine problem, look up *Bolivia* in these two publications. They will lead you to the most up-to-date information you can find.

1. In Bolivia, people of European descent have had more advantages than the native inhabitants of the country and their descendants. How does this compare with other countries you know about, including your own?

2. Look up Bolivia in *The Reader's Guide to Periodical Literature* and *Children's Magazine Guide*. Find articles that have been written about it recently. Report to your classmates about what has been happening in the last few months.

3. How has the geography of Bolivia affected its economy? What developments would make it a wealthier country?

More Things to Do — Activities

These projects are designed to encourage you to think more about Bolivia. They offer ideas for interesting group or individual projects for home or school.

1. Millions of the children of the world go to bed hungry, and many of these children are Bolivian. Ask your teacher or parents to help you find an organization that can use your help to feed people in Bolivia or other places, even your own town.

2. How far is Lake Titicaca from where you live? Using maps, travel guides, travel agents, or any other resources you know of, find out how you could get there and how long it would take.

3. How does your life compare with Porfirio's? Write an imaginary letter to him. Explain the ways in which you are the same or different.

4. If you would like a pen pal in Bolivia, write to these people:

International Pen Friends
P.O. Box 290065
Brooklyn, New York 11229-0001

Be sure to tell them what country you want your pen pal to be from. Include your full name and address and your age.

Index

"I am Porfirio Esteban." Adiós!